Writers and Their Familiars

A BOOK OF POSTCARDS   Photographs by Jill Krementz

Pomegranate

SAN FRANCISCO

Pomegranate
Box 6099
Rohnert Park, CA 94927

Pomegranate Europe Ltd.
Fullbridge House, Fullbridge
Maldon, Essex CM9 7LE
England

ISBN 0-7649-0372-1
Pomegranate Catalog No. A915

Pomegranate publishes books of
postcards on a wide range of subjects.
Please write to the publisher for more information.

Cover design by Shannon Lemme
Printed in Korea
06 05 04 03 02 01 00 99 98 97   10 9 8 7 6 5 4 3 2 1

Jill Krementz with Flour, a Maltese. "My daughter, Lily, and I got her when she was a tiny puppy and named her 'Flour' because she was light, white, and fluffy . . . and we knew she would rise to any occasion."

Photograph by Lily Vonnegut

As a young woman, Jill Krementz quickly established herself as one of America's most talented photojournalists, displaying a passionate and unique visual style. Throughout the 1960s, she worked as a reporter, columnist, and photographer for various New York–based publications—including the *New York Herald Tribune,* which hired her in 1964 as its first female (and youngest) staff photographer. She met her husband, Kurt Vonnegut, in 1970 when she photographed him shortly after the publication of *Slaughterhouse-Five;* they live in New York City with their daughter, Lily.

For the past three and a half decades, Krementz has moved back and forth between two worlds. On the one hand, there are her best-selling photo-essay books for young people, including the "Very Young" and "How It Feels" series, which have inspired and informed generations of children. On the other hand, there are her photographs of writers, which have grown into a massive—and unrivaled—photographic archive of contemporary literary figures comprising sessions with more than 1,500 writers. Her collection is not just a visual feast for modern book lovers; it will surely serve as an invaluable resource for future scholars, not unlike Carl Van Vechten's photographic collection of Harlem Renaissance writers of the 1920s and 1930s.

Uncompromising and thorough in her preparation, Jill Krementz brings to each session a familiarity with her subject's work. "I don't consider myself a photographer," she says. "I'm a photojournalist, since I generally photograph people in their environments. I try to see beyond the moment and into the subject. I want to show the private side of people without violating their privacy, and without being too intrusive." This sensitivity allows her to enter the individual writer's world unobtrusively, often capturing what John Updike, in his introduction to her most recent book, *The Writer's Desk* (Random House, 1996), calls "an ordering and a purging and a bringing into the light that which had been hidden an hour before." Her photographs, writes Updike, "in all their variety of milieu and demeanor, generally show people at peace in their settings, their activity, and their poses."

The most peaceful setting for many writers is one that includes the presence of a living nonhuman companion. While world literature is filled with tributes to the love and inspiration of familiars, perhaps Lord Byron put it best in an epitaph for his dog, Boatswain: "One who possessed beauty without vanity, strength without insolence, courage without ferocity, and all the virtues of man without his vices."■

Writers and Their Familiars

PHOTOGRAPHS BY JILL KREMENTZ

SAUL BELLOW with Moose, Brookline, Mass., March 1, 1997

Saul Bellow (b. 1915) is one of the century's great writers, author of the novels *Herzog* (1964) and *Humboldt's Gift* (1975) and winner of the 1976 Nobel Prize in literature. Sporting the top hat he wore to accept his Nobel Prize, Mr. Bellow says: "Moose is a fine black tom with a white throat who looks like a maitre d'hotel. He shares my bed daily. My siesta lasts for an hour. He sleeps some twenty hours a day." Once a castoff kitten discovered clinging to a screen door, Moose is now seven years old.

Pomegranate   Box 6099   Rohnert Park, CA 94927

Writers and Their Familiars

PHOTOGRAPHS BY JILL KREMENTZ

AMY TAN with Bubba Zo, New York, N.Y., April 26, 1996
Amy Tan (b. 1952) is author of the novels *The Joy Luck Club* (1990),
The Kitchen God's Wife (1991), and *The Hundred Secret Senses* (1995)
as well as children's books and essays. She lives in San Francisco and
New York with her husband and two Yorkshire terriers, Lilliput and
Bubba Zo. Bubba Zo, Tan says, is "my yappy little dog who often alerts
me to the presence of a muse in my writing room. Sometimes it turns
out to be the mail carrier or a construction worker next door. He also
guards against sloppy, boring writing."

POMEGRANATE   BOX 6099   ROHNERT PARK, CA 94927

Writers and Their Familiars

PHOTOGRAPHS BY JILL KREMENTZ

JOYCE CAROL OATES with Christabel, Princeton, N.J., February 7, 1997
Joyce Carol Oates (b. 1938) is a prolific writer of fiction (*Them,* 1969),
poetry, essays, and criticism as well as an editor for the *Ontario Review.* Her
most recent books are a novel, *Man Crazy* (1997) and a children's book
about a cat, *Come Meet Muffin!* Christabel, she says, is "a querulous but
beautiful calico Persian who helps her mistress write by meditating
intensely and by being nonverbal."

POMEGRANATE   BOX 6099   ROHNERT PARK   CA   94927

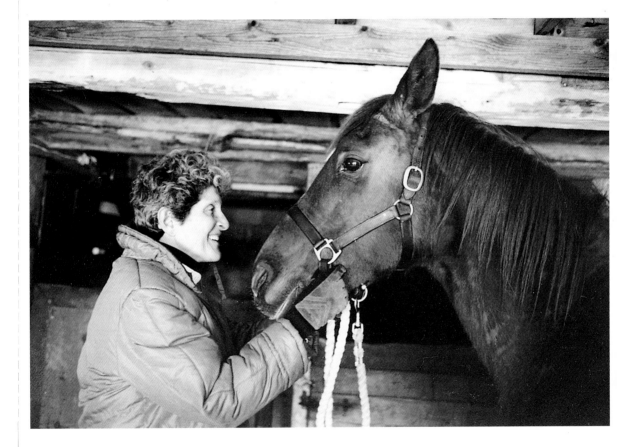

Writers and Their Familiars

PHOTOGRAPHS BY JILL KREMENTZ

MAXINE KUMIN with Deuter, Warner, N.H., February 13, 1997
Maxine Kumin (b. 1925) is a celebrated poet, novelist, and essayist,
author of *Looking for Luck* (1992) and *Women, Animals, and Vegetables*
(1994). She is also a prolific writer of children's books, many of which
feature animals as characters. Since 1963, she has run a working farm
in southern New Hampshire, where she lives with, among many other
familiars, a chestnut horse named Deuter. "My poetry, for the most
part, arises out of my everyday life here on the farm," Kumin says. "In
some strange way, my life with the horses and garden and New England
weather has become a metaphor for my work."

POMEGRANATE   BOX 6099   ROHNERT PARK, CA 94927

Writers and Their Familiars

PHOTOGRAPHS BY JILL KREMENTZ

EDWARD ALBEE with Poochi, Montauk, N.Y., August 9, 1976
Edward Albee (b. 1928) is a renowned playwright *(Tiny Alice, A Delicate Balance)* and opera librettist who, in 1996, received a Kennedy Center Honors Award for lifetime contribution to the nation's culture. Albee fondly recalls: "For eighteen years, Poochi [a Lhasa apso] guarded us all. He herded the Irish wolfhounds, and once he very gently chewed on the toes of a baby. He stopped when we asked him to."

POMEGRANATE BOX 6099 ROHNERT PARK, CA 94927

Writers and Their Familiars

PHOTOGRAPHS BY JILL KREMENTZ

OLIVIA GOLDSMITH with Frank and Matilda,
New York, N.Y., November 20, 1996
Olivia Goldsmith (b. 1955) is a novelist (*The First Wives Club,*
1992; *The Bestseller,* 1996; *Marrying Mom,* 1997) who describes
her subject matter as "female problems." Frank is a Siamese cat,
and Matilda is a beagle. "Writing is lonely," Goldsmith says, "so
it's nice to have the company of my dog and my cat. Matilda will
abandon me, but Frank is in for the long haul. He's all for a lap over
a laptop and a firm mouse over a track ball."

POMEGRANATE BOX 6099 ROHNERT PARK CA 94927

Writers and Their Familiars

PHOTOGRAPHS BY JILL KREMENTZ

WILLIAM STYRON with Aquinnah, Roxbury, Conn., April 29, 1979
William Styron (b. 1925) has written some of the most important novels
of our time, including *Lie Down in Darkness* (1951), *The Confessions
of Nat Turner* (1967), and *Sophie's Choice* (1979). Aquinnah, a golden
retriever, "had attributes that were nearly human, but she also possessed
all-too-human failings," Styron recalls. "For instance, when I taught her
how to drive, she insisted on staying on the left-hand side of the road.
So that ended her driving career, which made it all the better for our
wonderful daily walks together."

POMEGRANATE BOX 6099 ROHNERT PARK CA 94927

Writers and Their Familiars

PHOTOGRAPHS BY JILL KREMENTZ

ROBERT PENN WARREN with Frodo, Wardsboro, Vt., July 31, 1971
Robert Penn "Red" Warren (1905–1989) was a grand man of letters, an
author of novels (*All the King's Men,* 1947), essays, plays, and verse
(*Brother to Dragons,* 1953) who, in 1986, was named the first official Poet
Laurate of the United States. Frodo was his spaniel—named for a character
from a J. R. R. Tolkien novel—with whom he loved to take long walks
on his forty-acre farm. In Warren's poem "Rumor Verified," Frodo is
immortalized as "English cocker: old and blind / But if your hand / Merely
touches his head, / Old faith comes flooding back—and . . . / The paw
descends. His trust is infinite / In you. . . ."

POMEGRANATE BOX 6099 ROHNERT PARK CA 94927

Writers and Their Familiars

PHOTOGRAPHS BY JILL KREMENTZ

M. F. K. FISHER with Charlie, Sonoma, Calif., May 25, 1983
M. F. K. Fisher (1908–1992) grew up in California but moved to France
in 1929, using both settings—and the metaphor of food—to reflect on
and savor the details of life in works such as *The Art of Eating* (1954) and
A Cordial Water (1961). Charlie was Fisher's Siamese cat. She said, "I
think that elderly female writers hiding behind their Siamese cats should
be forbidden by law."

POMEGRANATE BOX 6099 ROHNERT PARK CA 94927

Writers and Their Familiars

PHOTOGRAPHS BY JILL KREMENTZ

WILLIAM F. BUCKLEY JR. with Rowley,
New York, N.Y., September 17, 1974

William F. Buckley Jr. (b. 1925) is the leading light of modern con-
servatism, founder and editor of *National Review,* and prolific author
of essays (*God and Man at Yale,* 1951), memoirs, and novels (*Mongoose,
R.I.P.,* 1988). Buckley recalls Rowley, his King Charles spaniel: "Rowley
(Rowley-Powley, when he was behaving) was my true love. He went with
me everywhere and posed engagingly, but only for certain photog-
raphers. Others he'd tell to check in during his office hours."

Pomegranate Box 6099 Rohnert Park CA 94927

Writers and Their Familiars

PHOTOGRAPHS BY JILL KREMENTZ

CAROLYN FORCHÉ with Coco, Rockville, Md., February 11, 1997
Carolyn Forché (b. 1950) has written three books of poems, including
The Angel of History (1994) and *The Country Between Us* (1982), and has
edited *Against Forgetting: Twentieth Century Poetry of Witness* (1993).
Her house, she says, is "gradually becoming an aviary: there are now a
pair of cockatiels and an Amazon blue-front parrot. Coco is a cockatiel
who enjoys shoulders, fingers, keyboards, and sunflower seeds. Coco has
a mate and may expect fledglings in the spring."

POMEGRANATE BOX 6099 ROHNERT PARK CA 94927

Writers and Their Familiars

PHOTOGRAPHS BY JILL KREMENTZ

TENNESSEE WILLIAMS with Sabbath, Key West, Fla., March 8, 1972
Thomas Lanier (Tennessee) Williams (1911–1983) created some of the
most memorable characters on the modern stage in plays such as *The
Glass Menagerie, Cat on a Hot Tin Roof,* and *A Streetcar Named Desire.*
Sabbath was a black cat whose predatory behavior (mauling lizards, in
particular) was a constant annoyance to Williams.

POMEGRANATE   BOX 6099   ROHNERT PARK, CA 94927

Writers and Their Familiars

PHOTOGRAPHS BY JILL KREMENTZ

MARGARET ATWOOD with Blackie, Toronto, Canada, June 25, 1994
Margaret Atwood (b. 1939) is an internationally acclaimed novelist and
poet whose best-known works are the subversively visionary novels *Life
Before Man* (1979), *The Handmaid's Tale* (1986), and *The Robber Bride*
(1993). An avid horticulturalist, she spent many hours with her feline
familiar, Blackie, in their Toronto garden.

POMEGRANATE   BOX 6099   ROHNERT PARK   CA   94927

Writers and Their Familiars

PHOTOGRAPHS BY JILL KREMENTZ

ROBIN COOK with Fluffy, Naples, Fla., February 21, 1997
Robin Cook (b. 1940) is an eye surgeon whose fifteen medical mystery
novels have thrilled and educated readers with their inside view of the
medical profession. His two most recent books, *Chromosome 6* (1997) and
Lethal Invasion (1997), were both best-sellers. Fluffy is a seventeen-year-
old bijon fusé. Cook says he and Fluffy "have a lot in common, including
the enjoyment of riding in a fast convertible with appropriate eye-
protective gear."

POMEGRANATE BOX 6099 ROHNERT PARK CA 94927

Writers and Their Familiars

PHOTOGRAPHS BY JILL KREMENTZ

STEPHEN KING with Marlowe, Bangor, Maine, July 20, 1995
Stephen King (b. 1947) is one of the world's most prolific and popular
writers, with more than twenty-five novels to his credit since 1974. His
most recent work, the serialized novel *The Green Mile* (1996), is an attempt
to duplicate Charles Dickens's feat of writing fiction to strict deadline.
Marlowe is a nine-year-old Welsh corgi. His owners say: "Marlowe doesn't
understand that he is a dog, or perhaps that we are not dogs. He eats
anything. Anything. His favorite trick is getting his teeth Waterpikked."

POMEGRANATE   BOX 6099   ROHNERT PARK CA 94927

Writers and Their Familiars

PHOTOGRAPHS BY JILL KREMENTZ

TERRENCE McNALLY with Charlie, New York, N.Y., May 18, 1974
Terrence McNally (b. 1939) is one of America's most important play-
wrights, author of *A Perfect Ganesh, Love! Valour! Compassion!,* and
Master Class. "Charlie was a great dog," McNally recalls. "He had a terrific
smile. When I told people I had a Cairn terrier, they would usually ask,
'What's that?,' and I would tell them that was the dog in *The Wizard of Oz.*
They would say, 'Oh, you mean he's like Toto,' and I would feel I had let
him down. Charlie was nothing like Toto. He was like Charlie."

POMEGRANATE   BOX 6099   ROHNERT PARK CA 94927

Writers and Their Familiars

PHOTOGRAPHS BY JILL KREMENTZ

RITA MAE BROWN with Ibid, Charlottesville, Va., February 17, 1997
Rita Mae Brown (b. 1944) is a novelist (*Rubyfruit Jungle*, 1973), poet,
screenwriter, and mystery writer (*Murder, She Meowed*, 1996) who clearly
knows when to let the cat out of the bag. "The cat is Ibid," she explains,
"an alley cat (fancy name: domestic shorthair) not yet one year old who is
being trained to follow in the paw-steps of her mentor, Sneaky Pie."

POMEGRANATE BOX 6099 ROHNERT PARK CA 94927

Writers and Their Familiars

PHOTOGRAPHS BY JILL KREMENTZ

MARK DOTY with Arden and Beau, Provincetown, Mass., August 6, 1996
Mark Doty (b. 1953) has, in his four books of award-winning verse (*My Alexandria*, 1993), created what one of his poems calls a "vast conjugation of the verb *to shine*." Arden is a flat-coated retriever, and Beau is a golden retriever. The poet describes his two familiars in *Heaven's Coast: A Memoir* (1996): "Heart's companions, good boys, eager, steady, always right in the present, at this moment's fresh edge."

POMEGRANATE   BOX 6099   ROHNERT PARK CA 94927

Writers and Their Familiars

PHOTOGRAPHS BY JILL KREMENTZ

ELIZABETH McCRACKEN with Tiger,
Somerville, Mass., November 29, 1996
Elizabeth McCracken (b. 1966) is the author of two books of fiction,
Here's Your Hat, What's Your Hurry (1992) and *The Giant's House:
A Romance* (1996). "Tiger's favorite place in the world is on my lap
when I'm trying to get work done," she says, "though she sometimes
sits on the top of my chair like a vulture, or an editor. She has only two
bad habits: she bites me every day, and she sometimes leaves her Ross
Perot catnip toy in the middle of my bed."

POMEGRANATE BOX 6099 ROHNERT PARK CA 94927

Writers and Their Familiars

PHOTOGRAPHS BY JILL KREMENTZ

P. G. WODEHOUSE with Jed, Remsenburg, N.Y., February 21, 1973
P. G. Wodehouse (1881–1975) was one of the most prolific writers of all
time, creator of immortal characters such as Bertie Wooster and Jeeves.
Devoted animal lovers, the Wodehouses owned many familiars, including
the dachshund Jed, and were active in the Westhampton branch of the
Bide-a-Wee Home Association, which cares for abandoned dogs and cats
until their adoption. The Westhampton branch is now called the P. G.
Wodehouse Shelter in commemoration of a generous donor.

POMEGRANATE   BOX 6099   ROHNERT PARK CA 94927

Writers and Their Familiars

PHOTOGRAPHS BY JILL KREMENTZ

KAYE GIBBONS with Huey Long, Raleigh, N.C., April 5, 1994
Kaye Gibbons (b. 1960) joined the front ranks of southern writers with
her first novel, *Ellen Foster* (1987), and has sustained her "good ear" and
"good heart" in three novels since, most recently *Sights Unseen* (1995).
Huey Long, she says, is "an ASPCA cat with an element of Siamese, who
sits as a sentinel while I'm working. My other three cats, Russell Long, Earl
Long, and Blaze Star, aren't as involved in the writing process."

POMEGRANATE BOX 6099 ROHNERT PARK CA 94927

Writers and Their Familiars

PHOTOGRAPHS BY JILL KREMENTZ

JOHN CHEEVER with Flora, Ossining, N.Y., October 1, 1971
Although he is renowned as a novelist (*The Wapshot Chronicle*, 1957),
John Cheever (1912–1982) made his most lasting mark in the modern
short-story genre, publishing his work in seven collections. Flora, a yellow
Labrador retriever, was named after Flora MacDonald by Cheever's son
Ben. In Sir Walter Scott's "Waverley" novels, MacDonald helped Bonnie
Prince Charles escape to the Isle of Skye.

POMEGRANATE BOX 6099 ROHNERT PARK CA 94927

Writers and Their Familiars

PHOTOGRAPHS BY JILL KREMENTZ

E. B. WHITE with Susy, North Brooklin, Maine, February 26, 1973
E. B. (Elwyn Brooks) White (1899–1985) was a longtime staff writer for
the *New Yorker* whose essays were known for their peerless clarity, wit,
and style. He also wrote three classic children's animal tales, *Stuart Little*
(1945), *Charlotte's Web* (1952), and *The Trumpet of the Swan* (1970).
While writing *Charlotte's Web*, White explained: "I like animals, and
it would be odd if I failed to write about them. Animals are a weakness
with me. When I got a place in the country I was quite sure animals
would appear, and they did."

POMEGRANATE BOX 6099 ROHNERT PARK CA 94927

Writers and Their Familiars

PHOTOGRAPHS BY JILL KREMENTZ

DONNA TARTT with Pongo, New York, N.Y., March 15, 1997
Donna Tartt (b. circa 1965) has published short stories and poetry
in *Harper's* and the *New Yorker*. Her debut novel, *The Secret History*
(1992), has been translated into more than twenty languages. Pongo,
according to Tartt, "takes on the shape of a pug dog when visitors call."

POMEGRANATE   BOX 6099   ROHNERT PARK CA 94927

Writers and Their Familiars

PHOTOGRAPHS BY JILL KREMENTZ

STEPHEN JAY GOULD, Cambridge, Mass., November 4, 1983
Stephen Jay Gould (b. 1941), a paleontologist and geologist by training,
possesses the rarest of combinations: a brilliant mind and an engaging
literary talent (*The Panda's Thumb,* 1980; *Dinosaur in a Haystack,*
1996). His familiars are this painted tyrannosaurus and "my beloved
fossil land snails, who lie still, never complain, look beautiful, and teach
us the numerous pathways of evolution."

POMEGRANATE BOX 6099 ROHNERT PARK CA 94927

Writers and Their Familiars

PHOTOGRAPHS BY JILL KREMENTZ

JAMES A. MICHENER with Burma (foreground) and Java,
Bucks County, Penn., July 9, 1974
James A. Michener (b. 1907) is renowned not only for his richly
researched novels (*Centennial,* 1974; *Chesapeake,* 1978) but also for
his generosity and humanity. He is seen here at the foot of a hill on
his property in Tinicum, Bucks County, Pennsylvania, where, he says,
"each afternoon Burma and Java would take me for a walk. They were
wonderful friends, and I loved them."

POMEGRANATE BOX 6099 ROHNERT PARK CA 94927

Writers and Their Familiars

PHOTOGRAPHS BY JILL KREMENTZ

KURT VONNEGUT with Pumpkin, New York, N.Y., February 17, 1982
Kurt Vonnegut (b. 1922) is one of America's best-loved writers,
creator of a world of biting satire and waggish wonder in such classics
as *Mother Night* (1966)—recently made into a film starring Nick Nolte—
Slaughterhouse-Five (1969), and *Bluebeard* (1987). His Lhasa apso's
tombstone reads: "Pumpkin loved sleeping." Vonnegut also loves
sleeping. "Naps are a great way to kill time," he says. "If I have nothing
to do, I'll take one. My dreams are so worthwhile. It's like Saturday
afternoon at the movies."

POMEGRANATE   BOX 6099   ROHNERT PARK CA 94927

Writers and Their Familiars

PHOTOGRAPHS BY JILL KREMENTZ

JACQUELINE MITCHARD with Pywackit, Madison, Wisc., June 10, 1996
Jacqueline Mitchard (b. 1952), though best known as an essayist, created a
literary sensation with her first novel, *The Deep End of the Ocean* (1996),
written as the result of a dream. "Pywackit, my sable ferret named for a
familiar—the Siamese cat used by Kim Novak to cast spells in the film *Bell,
Book, and Candle*—actually behaves more like a very small and addled
German shepherd," she says.

POMEGRANATE   BOX 6099   ROHNERT PARK CA 94927

Writers and Their Familiars

PHOTOGRAPHS BY JILL KREMENTZ

RUSSELL BANKS with Bodo, Princeton, N.J., April 21, 1995
Russell Banks (b. 1940) is an acclaimed writer of fiction whose novels include *Continental Drift* (1985) and *Rule of the Bone* (1995). "In Rumanian (or maybe it's Albanian), 'Bodo' means 'Ordinary Joe,' which suits him perfectly," Banks says of his familiar. "He's an American tabby, a true vernacular cat with a multicultural pedigree. He's expressive without being especially intelligent and thus is a boon companion when I'm doing solitary work."

POMEGRANATE BOX 6099 ROHNERT PARK CA 94927

Writers and Their Familiars

PHOTOGRAPHS BY JILL KREMENTZ

E. L. DOCTOROW with Becky, Gardiner's Bay, N.Y., August 3, 1975
E. L. (Edgar Lawrence) Doctorow (b. 1931) is a writer of conscience and
compassion who has explored the inner life of this century's history in
such novels as *Ragtime* (1975), *Loon Lake* (1980), *World's Fair* (1985),
and *The Waterworks* (1994). "Becky, a weimaraner, was bred to hunt,"
Doctorow says, "but she preferred swimming and cookouts in the
backyard."

POMEGRANATE BOX 6099 ROHNERT PARK CA 94927

Pomegranate Books of Postcards
on Photography, History, and Related Subjects

Pomegranate publishes books of postcards on a wide range of subjects.
Please write to the publisher for more information.

Witches and wizards have
always worked magic with
the help of "familiars,"
faithful spirits who have
assumed the shapes of animals,
and who are invariably nearby,
if you will look for them,
when spells are cast.

In this book of postcards, her fifth on the subject
writers, noted photojournalist Jill Krementz presen
thirty delightful images of people who write an
their familiars—the dogs, cats, and other cherish
animal companions who share their lives.

Pomegranate

CONTAINS THIRTY OVERSIZED POSTCA S

$9.95   A915   ISBN 0-7649-0 -1

7 17194 00915 2   9 780764 90 724